Decrypted

Poems for Mary Lou

by Mike Soper

Copyright 2012 by Michael T. Soper

Michael T. Soper

ISBN-10: 1479295469

ISBN-13: 978-1479295463

Copyright Registration: TX 7-568-319

Christmas Eve

On the night before Christmas, while eating
  Chinese,
and passing the noodles as calm as you
  please,
and chasing, with chopsticks, the egg in our
  soup,
we heard Chinese laughter; it sounded like
  croup.

And then, from the kitchen, we heard such
  a clatter,
we rose from our chairs to see what was the
  matter,
and whether our mother had fallen again,
when out of the kitchen came three
  Chinamen.

The first one was laughing, it shook his
  great tummy
and wobbled his earlobes. His breath, it was
  rummy.
Before we could finish counting his chins,
we knew this was Buddha, incarnate again.

The second was sterner, righteous yet
  loving,
and too dignified for such pushing and
  shoving.
With scrolls in his arms and his cap on
  his head,

we wondered if lawyers had lectures
   to dread.

The last one, a mortal, was dressed in blue
   cotton.
His smile was too cunning; his manners
   were rotten.
Like leading old animals out of a fable,
he dragged them and prodded them up to
   our table.

"We are three wise men; we follow a star.
Tonight it is cloudy, and so, here we are."
I knew this was hopeless; I knew I was
   beaten.
I muttered the requisite "So, have you
   eaten?"

That said, the Chinamen pulled up a chair.
Two started eating right then and right there.
Confucius regarded me, nodded approval,
then joined the others in dinner removal.

They ate up the shrimp and the double-
   cooked pork.
They finished our drinks, they ate with
   our forks.
They ate every lichee and mushroom
   and spore.
They beckoned each waitress; they ordered
   much more.

Out of the kitchen it steamed like a train:
lobsters and ducklings and bowls of lo mein,
beer, wine and liquor, Nectar of Bliss . . .
My father was livid: "Who's paying
    for this?"

Away from the table and outside I snuck.
Oh, what a bill ! I was going to get stuck.
I looked up; there wasn't a star in the sky.
I started to pray, either pray or I'd cry.

"Star of Wonder, Star of Light,
lead these wise guys on tonight.
Save a sinner, rescue dinner,
before my father starts a fight."

Who knows, for sure, if a prayer has been
    heard?
The traffic slogged on. A few breezes
    stirred.
A dark cloud above me shifted a bit,
and the old China Moon glowed right down
    through the slit.

I shivered. I still had some strength in
    my knees.
I walked to the table. I said, "Listen please,
it's Christmas, your long march must not be
    delayed.
I've just been outside; for your journey,
    I prayed.

The winds have been shifting and lifting
    the clouds.
The snow has stopped falling; the roads
    have been plowed."

Everyone stood. The great Buddha beamed.
He pulled a huge coin from his robe, and
    it gleamed.
He dropped it, and there was a flash of gold
    light.
We blinked, and The Three vanished into
    the night.

Everyone, *everyone*, joined in the feast,
the owner, the cooks, and six busboys,
    at least.
Our waitress picked up the gold coin,
    as she should.
She laughed as she chided us, "*those* guys
    tip good!"

Brood X

The 17-year Locusts of 2004

When Valentines come twice a year,
they echo all those lost Cicada,
they burrow from their little eggs
to kiss the roots of your tomato.

And what will grow, and what will die,
and what will live again? Good question.
And what we eat out on the deck
could test a little dog's digestion.

I look into those eyes of brown,
and pat a small dog on its head.
I look into your eyes of blue,
and thank my stars I don't see red.

Oh you, of all my kind, The Queen,
we met when we were seventeen.

Fred Fearing
ninety years old
Historic District
Elizabeth City, North Carolina
Columbus Day, 2004

Florence lives on Fearing Street.
Florence lives with Fred
in the house that she designed
after they were wed.

The tree has overgrown the house,
boxwoods big around,
a block away from Church Street
and Albemarle Sound.

Afternoons, Fred goes to greet
the boats that come each day.

Florence has a little rest
while Fred goes on his way.

Students, sometimes, come to note
what histories Fred keeps.
Florence does not interview;
Florence always sleeps.

But every Sunday, he goes
to the cemetery, then,
Florence goes along with Fred
to bring him home again.

Carida (Charity)

In 2004, I was a keyworker for the Combined
Federal Campaign. I distributed literature,
collected pledge cards, met some people,
and wrote some poems.

Carida suena, she dreams of the ballet.
The house lights dim, the curtains rise,
    a flute begins to play,
and another and another, answered by
    the strings,
now the costumed dancers come whirling
    from the wings.

A troupe of troops is marching up an
    avenue,
waving banners, roses, flags, the way that
    heroes do,

while silent groups of sailors gather to
  embark;
the avenue is brightly lit, the great warship
  is dark.

Ballet is her analogy, how moving pieces fit.
There isn't really music; she is not aware
  of it.
The story really matters, the whole world
  is a stage,
and the players, they are dancers, moving
  on a page.

I am interrupting, I bring her this year's
  book.
I ask her, "When you have a chance, why
  not have a look?"

But she replies, "I'm ready." She gives me
  a sly wink.
She says, "I have my favorites. Which ones
  do you think?"

"Oh me!" I cry. (I have to try.) She hands
  me back the book.
She says, "You look the numbers up."
  And so, I have to look.
And I realize I am watching someone give
  her heart away,
to dancers and musicians together, to ballet.

Joycelyn

I'm going to use my hand.
I'm going to close my fist.
I'm going to hold my pen.
I'm going to move my wrist.
I'm going to get a grip!
I'm going to rise and stand.
Here is my campaign pledge.
I signed it – with my hand.

Charlie

While John fills out his pledge card,
I see his photographs.
This looks like a one-dog show,
a dog that almost laughs.
First no bigger than his shoe,
then four times as big,
a dog that smells the flowers,
a dog that likes to dig,
the champion of hide & seek,
resting by the fire,
with eyes as soft as rain
with hair as soft as wire.
More than a dozen pictures,
just one caption on the wall:
I still love you Charlie

The Tree

Sometime, when you have a chance,
stop by and see our tree.
We've grown it from a potted plant
back in Building B.
We give it fertilizer,
bigger and bigger pots,
its leaves now brush the ceiling
in a half a dozen spots.

We hung a wind chime in it –
breezes never come.
We put a feeder in it –
humming birds don't hum.
No sky, no rain, no boundless earth,
if it was up to me,
(oh, why not be dramatic)
I would liberate the tree.

Really, just transplant it
to a wetter, warmer place,
with insects digging in the dirt,
and miles and miles of space,
and something in the sunshine
that is not in a grow-light,
and, just for decoration,
let it have the stars at night.

A Report from the Polls

At the Combined Federal Campaign
Pumpkin Carving Contest, 29 October 2004

I tried to pick a pumpkin,
I tried to cast my vote,
but "We are out of ballots."
Electioneers take note.
The ballots were delivered.
I asked, "May I have one?"
The Judge said, "Oh, take two or three,
elections are such fun!"
"One man, one vote!", I staunchly said.
"Some rules we must not bend."
"Oh lighten up! Buy Two!"
she said, "and give one to a friend."
"Buy?" I asked. "You're *selling* votes?"
"Yes. Every single one.
We are raising *money* here,
this is how it's done."
So, I bought two. I checked them out.
They didn't tell me much.
The ballots had no holes to punch,
they had no screens to touch.
No candidates were listed,
no parties indicated.
"How can I vote with this?" I cried,
and anxiously, I waited.
"You see these pumpkin-heads," she raged,
"the grandest in the land?

You take your little ballot,
you reach out with your hand,
you stuff it into the bag next to
the pumpkin of your choice,
and, if your pumpkin wins today,
by golly, you rejoice!"
I picked the nearest pumpkin.
I was shaking like a leaf.
Intimidation at the polls!
It was beyond belief.
I heard the Judge remarking
as I sadly walked away,
"So this is what it's coming to –
imagine Election Day!"

Octoberfest

Crimson fruits and berries
dangle from the trees,
attracting deer from out of the field,
the last of the summer's bees,
the wildest of the turkeys
landing with a flop,
the bravest of the bunnies
approaching hop by hop.
They nibble, they gobble,
they graze and chomp and chew,
digesting, fermenting,
the feast becomes a brew.

The little bees begin to buzz
and gently they expire.
The bunnies twitch,
the bunnies itch,
the bunnies are on fire.
The turkey periscopes his neck;
he is a winged giraffe.
The deer all stagger round and round,
and laugh and laugh and laugh.
"What is going on out here?
What is this commotion?"
The lady of the house has come
with all the wrath of Goshen.
"What are you doing in my trees?
What is going on?"
The deer escape, the turkey flies,
the bunnies all are gone.

Saint Bavo
Count Allowin , lived 589 to 654

I was once a royal knight
with lands to lease and foes to fight,
a wife to love me, oh, but then,
I fell into greed and sin.

A wandering preacher* came to town,
those I'd wronged had gathered round,
I was struck by what he said,
he asked me if my soul was dead.

He who gains by slavery,
only Christ can set him free.
Remorse was all there was of me,
hid away inside a tree.

Prayer by prayer, and tree to cell,
I re-emerged my tale to tell,
Christ can save more than a soul,
He can make a village whole.

A spirit now, the world I stride
with holy sisters* by my side.
Forgiven by the Lord above,
I bring your church his peace, his love.

*Saint Amand
*Saints Gertrude & Begga

Pork-Roll Turkey
It's a good thing.

We have had turkey sausage
and turkey lunch-meat ham,
but why not pork-roll turkey?
We never had that ma'am.

You could take some pork rolls
and carve them into parts:
wings and necks and gizzards,
drumsticks, wattles, hearts,
and, carefully, the part that

shows you if your bird's a tom
(we always like to know
if it's a dad or it's a mom).

Attach the wings and legs and things
with stainless turkey skewers,
then marinate your pork-roll bird
(away from Revenuers).
Then, stuff your bird! Yes! Stuff it
with celery, pretzels, onions.
Then stick it in the oven and
sit down and rest your bunions.

At 350, I guarantee,
this turkey will not fizzle.
It's going to roast, it's going to brown,
it's going to pop and sizzle.
Without a single mesquite chip,
this puppy will be smokin!
Turn your ventilator on
to save us all from chokin!

Down the hill in South Bend,
around the grill out back,
the firemen will chuckle,
"There goes Captain Jack."
Serve your bird with gravy,
a salad, and, oh my!
a vintage wine, some coffee,
and a slice of pretzel pie!

Southwest
To the tune of Mariah

They say out here a single steer
requires more barbed wire.
A cow in heat on down the street
can set his heart on fire.
Coyotes are a choir,
they sing about desire.

A single burro is a friend
to haul all you require.
A burro pair, a soulful stare
has consequences dire.
Your barn could catch on fire.
They sing about desire.

A studio is where you go
to watch the sun retire.
The moon comes up, a coyot pup
auditions for the choir.
His whole soul is on fire,
he sings about desire.

Desire !   Desire !
Oh when will we retire ?

A Possible Exception
14 February 2005

The moon re-energizes in your gaze.
Beasties beg and grovel for your praise.

Stars light up the heavens just for you.
So who am I, and what am I to do?

Industries supply your needs and wants.
Oceans bear you to romantic haunts.
Yours the shores of ice, the climes of wine.
So who am I to claim that you are mine?

Defended by armed forces and police,
Faiths compete to offer you their peace.
Preferred physicians keep you in their care.
What have I to offer but despair?

Oh tell me I don't matter, in the end,
except you might be lonely for a friend.

The Tucson Saga
Sung to the tune of Gilligan's Island

Now listen, couch potatoes,
and your TV will tell you
about two sisty-uglers and
some guy that they knew.

They thought they'd go to Tucson.
The Freeway runs quite well.
They opted for the scenery
on the Back Road from Hell.

The first and second mates
had navigated Italy;

the other guy sat in the back
because he couldn't see.

The first stop was an outlet mall,
a Lenox China shop.
There was a Red Hot Panty Sale --
the sisters wouldn't stop.

The Superstition Mountains
rose against a hazy sky.
Apache Spirits cursed them
as their rental car rolled by.

They headed south for Florence
and the prisons of the state;
beside the road, escapees
were lying low in wait.

Hohokums built a tower
and irrigation streams.
They disappeared but they'll be back
to haunt you in your dreams.

They stopped at a McDonalds
for burgers, cokes and fries;
they at it IN the rental car –
Dust Devils filled the skies.

They stopped a while in Tombstone,
in Big Nosed Kate's Saloon.
It smelled just like old Hull's Hotel.
They had to pee real soon.

There hadn't been a prostitute
in Bisbee town in years.
The miners saw the sisters and
they gave three mighty cheers.

They waited for their supper
till the moon rose in the north,
then, from the sewers, freak Kazooers
came Marching Forth.

The Copper Queen was dubious.
They shivered in their beds
while psychopathic monsters
stomped on bodies overhead.

The copper isn't worth a cent,
but someone smelt a gain:
The miners sue the tourists
who derail their train.

The Saints at the Old Mission
have lost a head or two.
If you don't make an offering,
then saints preserve you.

Another friend preceded them,
their rendezvous confused:
They should have been in Switzerland,
eating cheese fondues.

They were beguiled by pseudo-pigs,
with not so pseudo turds –

they stood there like five idiots,
ignoring humming birds.

The First Mate was a Botanist,
her plant identities
were just about the opposite
of what they ought to be.

The Creosote was festooned
with hanging Mistletoe.
The Other Guy said, Hey let's kiss.
The Second Mate said, No.

They hiked Sabino Canyon.
The cottonwoods were green.
A river runs right through it
to the nearest Dairy Queen.

The Old Prospector found
the biggest ruby ever seen.
He cashed it for a Heath Bar Breeze
at the Dairy Queen.

They drove back on the Freeway.
Their wanderlust was spent.
They'd seen enough in half a State
for half a Continent.

But if you go to Tucson,
be sure to take along
some other guy to sit in back
and write a silly song.

Junk Mail

14 August 2005

When Valentines come twice a year
they fall in with the other mail,
between an Overseas Adventure
and the next Hecht's weekend sale.

And would you say that all my love
is worth more than the merchandise?
Or would you say that here with me
is better than a paradise?

And what about that Singles ad?
And what about that model male?
Doesn't mother stay with dad?
Doesn't he look weak and pale?

Or did you even notice me
among such glossy company?

Gladie is Ninety

Gladys Elsie Mock, 31 October 1915

If you want to know someone's birthday,
    ask Gladie.
Newborn, in-law, great grandparent –
    gone long ago,
Gladie will know.

Her own birthday is easy, it's Halloween.
She was born third, after Helen and Mary,
still no boy, and too many cows to milk,
finally, John and Richard,
briefly, Marjorie and Donald,
happily, Peggy, amen.

Gladie went to school,
she learned and learned.
Gladie returned to school,
she taught and she taught,
every child in town.
This is a nice town.

Gladie keeps the Family Tree,
advances genealogy
forwards, backwards, sideways,
page after page.
There are Beachs and Brumbaughs
and Replogles running through it,
like threads through a quilt.

Gladie married a railroad man.
They never left home.
They retired; found a winter place,
down on the Gulf, out of the snow,
near Dick & Hope, then Mary & Harry.
There's an old railroad station
in a park with palm trees
at the end of the line.

Here, the great circus comes
to rest and renew itself,
the sun sets in the water,
seashells come to the shore.

Spring brings Chet & Gladie
back to Morrison's Cove.
There are new nieces and nephews,
new husbands and wives.
Gladie adds them to the Tree.
Summer comes.
There are no finer farms on earth.
There is no sweeter corn, no better pie.

A cove is a valley up high in the hills.
When you live in a cove, twilight lingers.
And still, the seasons pass.
The harvest is over, the trees have turned.
It is Gladie's birthday,
time, again, to go South.

Happy Birthday, Gladie.
Be safe, stay warm, be well.
Always come home.

No Ode to Beau

Beau has not inspired a poem;
there is no *Ode to Beau*.
He's white and brown, his ears stick up,
there's not much more to know.

His legs are long, he walks too fast,
his tail curls to his right.
He licks my face, he licks my hair,
he licks my ears all night.

Beau is mean to his sister;
his sister indulges Beau.
She follows along like a faithful dog
wherever he wants to go.

He wants to go to the ends of the earth,
or at least to the ends of Burke.
He wants to walk all of the time,
especially after work.

Beau eats plain dry dog food,
and, sometimes, boiled peas,
and grapes and cheese and corn-on-the-cob,
for which he has learned to sneeze.

He also eats stuffed animals;
he eats their beating hearts.
I squeak a bit, sometimes, myself,
when Beau and I are apart.

Of course, he lifts his leg to pee.
He has killed a plant or two.
His mother says, "No more boy dogs."
Oh Beau, what will I do?

Your Sister, to the Rescue

So, your sister bought a burro
for your husband. Well, that's nice,
but that amount of detail
for a poem won't suffice.
So, I called her up and asked her,
Does this burro have a name?
She replied, So far, he doesn't,
but he has a claim to fame.

Seems a Mary named Maria
rode the burro into town.
There were shepherds with a little flock
grazing all around,
and a Joseph and a Padre
and a lovely baby child --
everyone in costume
acting meek and mild.

Seems the mayor came to meet them
with a sheriff and a cop,
and he whipped out a Court Order
and he told the family, Stop !
So they stopped. But he kept coming,
till he got up in their face;
he said, Jesus cannot come here
-- not to *any public place.*

Maria, she dismounted
and sadly walked away.
She told her little baby boy,

Sorry, not today.
Joseph and the shepherds
rounded up the sheep,
while their Padre stood there shaking,
trying not to weep.

What about this burro?
the sheriff asked, then said,
I can fix this burro,
I can shoot him dead.
The Padre barely answered;
replied without much hope,
We thought about Palm Sunday . . .
The mayor just said, Nope.

Then your sister, who was watching
who was only passing by,
told the officers, The burro's mine.
He's mine. Don't even try.
And she told the little Padre,
Father, you will get my note.
And she told the mayor and the sheriff,
You *won't* get my vote.

Then your sister rode the burro home.
(Someday, she'll get the car.)
She tied him in her stable,
underneath a big bright star.
And she wrote you and your husband:
I have a gift for you.

But you're going to have to name him
-- maybe Bullet. That would do.

Groundhog's Day

The world revolves to a certain point
or else has lost its way,
and I have surfaced topside,
just at the break of day,
to take a fix on the morning star
and mark the rising sun,
and to see through the fog
or the rain or the snow
if Springtime has begun.

I take my cosmic bearings
and ponder them alone.
Far have I tunneled underground
through Pennsylvania stone.

Better to go fishing
in a shower full of mirth
than to try to rush the seasons
or try to tilt the earth.
Better to go camping now,
and sing a campfire song,
than wait for warmer weather
while the shadows grow too long.

Code Yellow
on the eve of shoulder surgery

If I were an old orangutan
and you were my faithful mate,
I'd build my nest down on the ground,
and clutch my stick and wait.
The sun would set in heaven
as tigers circle round.
You would drop me a banana;
I would weep without a sound.

If I were old and injured
and panthers came at night,
I would roar just like a tiger
to give those beasts a fright.
But that would bring more tigers,
looking for a meal.
You would drop them some bananas
they would not know how to peel.

If I were old and broken
with tigers closing in,
you'd go swinging through the jungle
to find some hunting men.
You would offer them bananas
to come and rescue me.
You would lead them through the jungle,
swinging tree to tree.

If I were old and desperate,
fighting with one arm,

you'd come roaring back to me
to rescue me from harm.
You'd bring hunters and bananas
and a little dog or two.
I don't much like bananas,
but I'm very fond of you.

Bolognese !

Sung to a Neapolitan Melody

In divinity school, the first verse begins:
Last night, I stayed up late to meditate.

Our praise begins with garlic that you braise
for Bolognese. A glass we raise
to Bolognese.

Of noodles, wearing hardly anything
while they're boiling,
of nudes we sing.

Your sauce wins our applause,
it is so very nice.
Such subtle spice !

Salad ! with spinach leaves
and dressings on the side,
so you decide.

Grated cheeses, kisses for the Cook,
better recipes than from a book,
and would you look how good you look !

You'll get more than praise for
  Rigatoni Bolognese.

Blue Statue

Holden Beach, North Carolina

A heron stands in the study.
His head is bowed in thought.
He thinks of what he hasn't.
He thinks of what he ought.
He listens to the ocean,
so different from the bay.
He ought to be out fishing,
but he's wishing he could stay.

Counterparts

14 August 2006

When valentines come twice a year,
they do not come as a surprise.
Still, I thought you ought to hear
how bright you shine; you light the skies.

I am darkness; you are the moon,
a ship aglow upon the sea.
You are the lyrics and the tune.
I am the hill; you are the tree.

I am a submarine to ride.
I am hunger; you are the cook.
You are my home in a world too wide.
You are the subject of my book.

And oh my girl, my bride, my wife,
you are the love that saves my life.

Well, Well, Well
(to the tune of Turkey in the Straw)

Well, my name is Mary, and I'm still not
     three,
and my Nanna Nancy came to care for me,
and she brought her sister, Mary Lou, along,
and they entertain me with a little song.

Dad has a necktie, Mary has a bib.
Mom has a pillow, Mary has a crib.
Nanna has a sister, I do too,
mine is Anna, her's is Mary Lou.

Well, it's wintertime, so we play inside,
and I ride my little horse I like to ride,
and I tickle my sister 'till she hics right up;
then she has her bottle, and I drink my cup.

Mary's gonna run and Anna's gonna crawl.
Mary's gonna climb and Anna's gonna fall.
Anna takes a nap, and I will too,
and so will Nanna and Aunt Mary Lou.

Well, my nap is over and I'm in the tub,
and a warm wet washcloth is a good
   backrub,
and a pin~a colada is a shweet shampoo,
but I can't lay down in here, I'm only two.

I like cheese, and Anna eats mush.
I like peas, and Anna eats slush.
I'll eat a cookie, I'll eat two.
She doesn't really eat, she cannot chew.

Well, our dinner's over, and we
   watched TV,
and it's bedtime for Anna, but it's not for me
'cause my mom reads to me from a picture
   book,
and if you play mamma, you are on the
   hook.

Tell me about your little dog, Beau.
Tell what we'll do, after I grow.
Say you'll come and stay with me
the next time Mom & Dad sail off to sea.

Fairy Queen

She smiles at small dogs.

Behold, the Queen of the Fairies,
enthroned upon your lawn,
humming in the moonlight,

welcoming the dawn,
settling the evening,
bathing in the rain,
snuggling beneath the snow
'till sunshine comes again.

Shucking the Seventh Oyster

Of all the wounds throughout the land,
yours is the deepest in the hand,
through the thumb and into a bone;
your blood dripped from the telephone.
But more than deep and more than wide,
this cut, I know, was to your pride:

because your oyster knife was new,
and the oyster was a gift to you,
and you stand right there and you grind
   the meat
where confidence and skills compete.

Who doesn't know that a butcher's knife
is a part of himself, like his pipe or his wife?
Shuck an oyster ? Clean a fish ?
Any bloody time I wish !

Well, tell your friend, from me to you,
there must be a knack to what we do.
Shuck my oysters, I'll grind your meat.
It's called respect; we don't compete.

And the next time I bring oysters home,
they will be shucked, in styrofoam.

Five Golden Rings

Steve shopped on the Internet.
His bids were swift and bold.
He picked and clicked, he triple bet,
he won three rings of gold:
a ruby set with diamonds,
a topaz barely blue –
but Starr lives on the Nevernet;
She waits. She waits for you.

Halfway through December,
Steve received the rings.
He brought them in, he showed them round,
we talked of girlish things:
of how an emerald goes as well
with casual clothes or gown.
Starr did not avert her eyes.
Her hopes in you abound.

Christmas is the season
when wise men bring a gift,
but neither frankincense nor myrrh
averts a marriage rift.
We need to do what Steven did
to win a ring of gold:

go log on the Internet,
and let our bids be bold!

Serving Papers up the Hill of Perpetual Adoration

Flapping grimly through the endless snow,
as the frozen river fades from sight,
Cupid struggles up the hill below;
evening vespers lift him through the night.

A fortress, built of brick encased in stone,
stands illuminated at the top –
impregnable but taxable – alone.
Cupid does not brake, he does not stop.

He crashes, belly-flops, against the door,
and beats it with his hands and wings
    and feet.
Nancy opens up to help the poor
naked creature in out of the sleet.

"Cupid ! Have you brought a card for me ?
a Valentine ? from my Dearest Heart ?"
"An Injunction, from the Holy See.
Sorry, nothing from your dear old fart."

"The Holy See ! Oh pray, what do they
    say?"
"They say you've got to stop slaying deer.
The deer are innocent, and anyway,

where do you think you are ? on some
   frontier ?"

"I told the Sister, 'We've been **sleighing,**
   dear.'
Now do you have a card for me, or not?"
"Not from the ecclesiastic court.
I just gave you everything I've got."

So, Nancy pitched him out into the snow.
He could have froze to death.
She does not know.

Just Warming Up

We worry, when the winter is warm,
that plants will bloom to die in a storm,
that birds and beasts too soon will mate;
we hope exuberance will wait.

The fox comes out and prowls the hill;
he gives the squirrels an awful thrill.
And birds that should have flown away
trill in the trees ten hours a day.

The gardens try to bud and leaf.
Crocus bloom beyond belief.
Doggies nap less than they should.
Even the snow is pure and good.

And treasured, the whole winter long,
you are my thrill, my mate, my song.

Turkey in the Yard

to the tune of Turkey in the Straw

On the top of the hill off Dragoon Trail,
there's a big stone house with no fence rail,
no water trough, no rows to till,
but the lawn grows greener than a dollar bill.
Chorus:
Deer in the cornfield, turkey in the yard,
Jack at the window standin' guard,
pop goes the popgun, squeal goes the
   squirrel,
songbirds rise in a dancin' twirl.

When the raccoon comes to wash his mouse
in the waterfall by the big stone house,
Jack grabs his gun and takes his aim;
the coon goes runnin' off a little lame.
Alternate Chorus:
Coons in the fountains, turkeys in the trees,
hawks sailing circles up in the breeze,
sunlight, moonlight, shadows in the yard,
Jack's at the window, he's a standin' guard.

When the grandsons come to ride the sled,
they eat their popcorn and they go to bed.
If they climb the curtains or they bang
   the walls,
Jack goes to get the gun, and silence falls.
Chorus:

When a turtle comes to warm his shell
by the fire pit in the popcorn smell,
if he sits on a marshmallow, toasted
   and gooed,
then he'll sit right tight 'till he comes
   unglued.
Scatological Chorus:
Have you considered some little dog,
chasing the squirrels, finding a frog?
What would Jack in the window do
when his dog deposited a pile of pooh?

When a possum hangs from the Old
   Pooh Tree,
swelling, shrinking, rhythmically,
a shadow in the lamplight, Jack takes aim
and sends that possum on to Notre Dame.
Chorus:

When the nuns hear the guns on the top
   of the hill,
they pray all day, "Let the guns be still!"
With varmints a-grazin' there is no end
   to war
but the lawn grows greener than it
   grew before.
Chorus:

When granddaughters come to spend
   the day,

Nanna Nancy puts the gun away.
No little animals will come to harm
while the girls are watching on the
   green grass farm.
Chorus:

I shouldn't tease my brother Jack.
Each new kindness brings a fresh attack.
But there's nuns at the bottom and guns
   at the top,
I just can't find a quiet place to stop.
Chorus:
What do the turkeys gobble about?
Why do the squirrels chatter and shout?
Why do the deer all run away
when they hear the popgun and the
   fiddle play?

Arizona Mountains

to the tune of Que Sera Sera

When I was just a blushing bride,
I asked my husband, where shall we head?
Shall we go west where the sun goes to bed?
Here's what my husband said:
We'll need dirt, my love,
the moon is more far than near.
A truckload won't do, I fear.
We'll need lots of dirt.

When I had had enough of dirt,
I asked my builder, when will you start?
He looked at me like I'm out of my head.
Here's what my builder said:
You'll need dirt, my dear.
A flood could wash right through here,
as strong as your husband's steer.
You'll need lots more dirt.

One night, I climbed up on my dirt,
sat on my camp stool under the stars.
I heard coyotes cry on a hill,
and I can hear them still:
Once we were like you.
We dreamed of a mountain view,
out under the moon and stars.
Now we live like moles,
in our mountain holes,
in our piles of dirt.

Emma Jumps Rope

Emma eats this and Emma eats that,
Emma eats vegetables with rat,
roasted peppers, hot and sweet,
how many rats does Emma eat?

Emma eats that and Emma eats this,
Emma eats holes from cheeses Swiss,
holes that smell like stinky feet,

how many holes does Emma eat?

Emma eats those and Emma eats these,
Emma eats ratatouille with peas,
wrinkled little peas so sweet,
how many peas does Emma eat?

Emma eats these and Emma eats those,
she eats pickled piggy toes,
pickled in vinegar and brine,
on how many does she dine?

Emma jumps ropes and Emma skips whips,
Emma jumps chains and never trips,
hops up and down on the devil's hump,
how many times does Emma jump?

Emma vaults fences, hurdles mud,
Emma leaps over fire and flood,
Emma has helpers, Emma has hope,
how many angels hold the rope?

Fading Away

She washed a towel for drying dogs,
a bright magenta red.
She bleached it with my underwear.
"I washed your stuff", she said.

After a while, my underwear
has lost its charm, I know,
and stains wash out,

and stains wash in.
It is the afterglow.

Beware, dog !
to the tune of Mariah

Los hombres hum and guitars strum
around a little fire.
The plywood gutters green and blue,
like emerald or sapphire.
Our dog is nearly napping,
her tail is gently flapping.

The sprinklers aren't connected yet,
they cost a lot of money;
supposed to keep the plywood wet
in a land that's mostly sunny.
Our visitors are going,
they've left their campfire glowing.

Out West, it seems, the turquoise gleams
in bracelets made of copper.
I'm going to tie the dog outside
to keep some jeweler proper.
Our dog is going to stop her,
or I'll go out and bop her!

By doggy! Start learning
to keep the house from burning!

She's in Chicago
14 February 2007

When Valentines come twice a year,
they find a gloomy, windy day.
They find a week when you're not here,
and even birds have flown away.

The dogs and I, we dine alone,
a can of tuna fish to share.
We listen for a ringing phone,
and gaze upon your empty chair.

While half a continent away,
you hold the daughters of your niece,
and tell them it's a Special Day,
and give them each a kiss apiece.

The dogs and I do not believe
it's better to give than to receive.

Reconstruction

From seventeen tree stumps in a row,
the ghosts of cherry blossoms blow.

Oh rising sun ! Oh morning breeze !
Welcome, sons of cherry trees !

Lost Hideaway
14 August 2007

When valentines come twice a year,
arriving at a House for Sale,
the odds are worse than they appear,
a warm reception could prevail.

Cupid takes his place in line,
behind the dirty carpet steamer,
the locksmith, the assorted nine
inspectors, and the clogged pipe reamer.

I am something of a dreamer.
I am your devoted spouse.
I am a romantic schemer,
even in an Open House.

I'll catch you with adoring eyes,
and whisper, You are *such* a Prize.

The Mirror
14 February 2008

Six feet one inch off the floor,
fourteen inches screw to screw,
what brazen hooks would dare to hold
the looking glass reflecting you?

Your hair, like mine, is getting long.
You do not wear a hat today.

The speakers are without a song.
Your clothes are suitable and gay.

The neighbor lady rings the phone
and off you go to have high tea.
The dogs and I are left alone;
they'd rather be with you than me.

We have our paperwork and chores;
the dogs proceed without complaint.
I'll need your help with cabinet doors.
I work, as quiet as a saint.

Till passing by your dresser, and
the bare wall where your glass should be,
I thought I saw it hanging there.
I thought I saw you watching me.

I saw my high school valentine
become my war-time sweetheart bride.
We did not have this mirror then.
Why aren't I standing by your side?

I stepped to where your mirror waits,
leaning on a corner wall.
I saw my legs below the knees,
and two small dogs, and that is all.

The Prognosis

The man with seven nipples returned
   as from a war.
His wife was all concern-ed, she met him
   at the door.
She asked, What's the prognosis ? He said,
   They wouldn't say,
except go see our lawyer, and make my Will
   today.

He gave unpublished poems to the local
   League of Arts.
He gave his stamp collection to a couple of
   old farts.
He gave two score devotions to a missionary
   nun.
But he wouldn't give his wife away,
   not to anyone.

The man with seven nipples came marching
   through the door.
He tore the cathode nipples off, and threw
   them on the floor.
He said, They were mistaken, we do not
   have to part.
It's only you that's causing this throbbing
   in my heart.

Vivo pensando de tu.

I live thinking of you.

14 August 2008

When valentines come twice a year,
they signify that life goes on;
we wipe away another tear,
we rise up to another dawn.

What energies I must exhaust,
what parts I lose along the way,
they are, you know, forever lost;
they don't return another day.

Yet here you stand to see me home,
affection in your eyes and voice,
who could, yourself, the whole world roam;
you stay with me of your own choice.

What's left of me belongs to you,
and will, no matter what you do.

Pasquotank Boulevard

Out in the shade of the hedges,
where robins are plying for worms,
Bobo is leading and frisking,
and I am still coming to terms.

Fresh morning breezes are blowing;
tiny birds flutter and tweet.

Gardeners are needlessly mowing
the verge of the long empty street.

Out on the Capital Beltway,
commuters are locked in their grid.
Employers are making good offers,
and, God help me, one of them did.

I'm mentally packing a suitcase.
This week, I rejoin the crew.
But oh my Beau, my darling,
I'd rather be walking with you.

The Dirge of the Barnacle Biddy
to the presumptuous tune of
The Wreck of the Edmund Fitzgerald

There's a song of three notes
that the men in pea-coats
try to sing through their frozen mustaches.
And they sing it aloft,
though they sing it so soft
it gets lost in the wind and the splashes.

There's a pie that they bake
on the shores of the lake,
but they fill it with eels that are smelly.
If you don't like the pie,
they suggest that you try
toasted bread spread with sturgeon-egg jelly.

For fresh caviar,
you don't have to go far,
hook a worm and just chuck it over.
If a big sturgeon hits
she could shake you to bits;
pray to God that she isn't a rover.

For that was the fate
of the skipper and mate
and the crew of the Barnacle Biddy.
She towed them around,
round the harbor and town,
'till the sailors and townies grew giddy.

Then she headed up-lake,
for her un-laid eggs sake,
to unite with her monstrous man-fish.
And they heard the fish cry,
'I'll be filleted if I
will relinquish my fry for a sandwich!'
So she hauled them away
for a month and a day
'till they thought that she'd drag 'em
    all under.
Wouldn't you bet your life
they'd have taken a knife
and just cut the fish line asunder?

But a great epic lay
isn't written that way,
it requires a crew that's heroic,

and witty and wise,
and without any guise,
and more than unreasonably stoic.

So they waited too late
'till the big fish's mate
overwhelmed their sonar recorder.
When he flopped up on deck
he was bigger than heck,
there was no way to repel that boarder.

And the cabin was crushed,
and the sailors were mushed,
and he thrashed and crashed just like
    thunder.
And his big mate below,
she continued to tow,
and the Barnacle Biddy slid under.

There's a song of three notes
that they hum in their throats,
it's *The Dirge of the Barnacle Biddy*:
How they paid for their ride,
and they sank and they died,
and even their song is a pity.

Belle
14 August 2009

When Valentines come twice a year,
they come with stubby little tails,

with chocolate face and brindling,
with ears as big as Dumbo sails.

She brings us squeaky teddy bears
or, sometimes, just a chewed-off ear.
Thank God she doesn't bring us snakes
when Valentines come twice a year.

She does not give you all her love.
She tries to spread the love around,
though Tigger wants to bite her nose,
and Bobo thinks that she's a clown.

So, I will watch this dog with you
to see what puppy love can do.

Atop Old Seville

Take a deep breath, Francisco,
and now exhale your fear.
The crushing street lies far below,
but your work has been hoisted up here.
Here is Our Lady's angel,
the fairest child of your hands.
Set her above the cathedral
and the city and the land.

She will be the first to see
the ships come sailing home,
and the pilgrims come and the pilgrims go
along the road to Rome,

bulls enter arenas,
gold removed from the ships,
and the people come to the chapels below
with prayers upon their lips,
or the drought before the harvest
and the moon begin to wane,
and the dead hauled out of the city
when the plague comes round again,
or the wind that fans the fire
that will burn the plague away,
and the slow repopulation,
child by child, and day by day.

She will stand the ages;
you will totter on your feet.
Life is disappointment.
Dreams invite defeat.
Here is your consolation,
you will sit below this place,
and close your dim half-blind old eyes,
and remember your angel's face.

Jingle Belle

There's a big dog loose in the wood.
There's a rumble of wings in the air.
Let the great heron die where he stood !
Let the fox and the rabbits beware !

There's a big dog tracking the deer,
harrowing, gobbling mice.
Let the little moles tremble with fear,
and pray for a cover of ice !

Lunch at Nickalena's
Hertford, North Carolina

The building is older than we are,
I'm guessing by seventy years.
The stairs are getting creaky,
the windows have permanent smears.
The table cloths are plastic,
the service stainless steel,
nor linen nor lace nor silver
would change the way we feel.

The young cook stands like a mountain,
the waitresses half his size.
The mothers of the waitresses
supply the cakes and pies.
The local clerks and shoppers
assemble and say Hi.
Sometimes we say hello here,
sometimes we say goodbye.

Across the street by the courthouse,
under a couple of trees,
a monument to Catfish
rests in the shade and the breeze.

Born and raised and died here,
he played the game away.
And out of Yankee Stadium,
I'm on the road today.

Local hero, James "Catfish" Hunter
pitched for the New York Yankees.
Natives of Hertford call the Albemarle
Plantation "Yankee Stadium" because of
all its retirees from the north.

Lonely

Another sunset on a crowded road.
A truck insists that I keep up the pace.
A sky so lovely that I might have slowed,
but I'm denied the moment and the space.

And, every mile, a mile away from you.
Our phones impart remoteness to your
    voice.
One final job, I have to see it through.
I miss you, Boo. I do regret my choice.

But if the trucker doesn't run me down,
I think that I could replicate this sky
above us on the Albemarle Sound
or elsewhere, if we travel by and by.

And let this be the last time that I sign
myself, "with love, your lonely valentine".

Tiger Tea

14 February 2010
Chinese New Year 4708

When Valentines come when they should,
I hope it's not by ambulances.
Even if the roads are good,
I'll carefully assess our chances.

Cupid flies at six-o-eight.
Straightaway he's coming hither.
He's coming nude – I must relate,
he says he's "feeling all-a-quiver".

The Carriage House still doesn't know
what, exactly, they'll be serving.
Nevertheless, that's where we'll go:
we planned it, so we can't go swerving.

Venison, with Tiger Tea,
would make you dear, this year, to me.

New Verses for *Grandma's Lye Soap*

Someone here, an engineer,
dug a deep well 'till his water was clear.
He added some flakes of Grandma's
  Lye Soap,
now his water foams like beer.

You know someone, sometimes a dumb one,
but well-intended, excessively neat.
He cleaned his crawl-space with the lye
    soap,
he has the deepest basement on the street.

Lovely Laura, from Tuscarora,
has a compulsion for washing her yacht.
She scrubbed her poop deck with the
    lye soap
and you will not find a dirty spot.

Tree, R. I. P.
(Just grow watermelons!)

The list of trees that have died here
is a long sad list indeed.
It makes you stop and wonder
where the dogs of midnight peed.
I suppose you would have noticed
if the deer chewed off the bark,
but do you know where the possums go
to hang themselves in the dark?

If an itchy bear scratched his back right
    there
would a sapling survive?
Had we gathered there and all prayed
    a prayer
would a tree be left alive?

In your bitter grief, did you lift a leaf,
tell those beetles where to go?
Will there ever be a canopy
of shade where impatiens grow?

Along Meherrin River Drive
the tadpoles grow to frogs.
The seeds of the Loblolly Pine
grow into mighty logs.
From leveled lots, the homes rise up
cathedral ceiling high.
But every tree you plant here,
well – it does just make you cry.

Too Hot

14 August 2010

When valentines come twice a year,
they don't elicit extra heat;
they try to be like ice cream cones,
melting, but still cool and sweet.

You agree to some romance
if we can find a little shade,
a little breeze, a little squeeze
more lemon in the lemonade.

I lay back and I close my eyes;
the ceiling fan is gently rocking.

The big dog climbs up in my lap;
her body heat is scorching, shocking.

Keep me straight and keep me strong;
feed me lightly, keep me sober.
I will love you all night long,
slowly, gently – in October.

Your Birthday
September 2010

If you had never been born,
and there weren't any stars in the sky,
I certainly would be forlorn,
but I wouldn't be certain just why.

I would be just as lost as before
with no way to get through the night.
If I lived to be seventy-four,
nothing would ever be right.

My sons wouldn't have the right genes.
My home wouldn't have the right touch.
My meals wouldn't have the right taste.
My bank account wouldn't have much.

The poor moon would just drag along
without any sparkles around;
and something else terribly wrong:
It wouldn't reflect on The Sound.

The prospect was getting so bleak,
The Good Lord, He had to relent:
He sprinkled the heavens with stars,
and look at the angel He sent!

Homecoming

14 August 2011

When valentines come twice a year,
they greet you like a long-lost dog.
Every blue bird sings a cheer;
a serenade sings every frog.

A sign they've posted, right out front,
ironically reads Welcome Back.
And every door will open wide
while Belle is searching for a snack.

The rhythmic pounding of the surf
faded, faded every mile,
until you stood on your home turf
a long, long way from Emerald Isle.

But here is your adoring throng,
and one who's loved you, much and long.

The Smart Phone Blues
(a rap)

You said we'd be alone
but then you brought your phone.
It beeps and boops and bops;
it hardly ever stops.

It has a bunch of aps
you do with finger taps.
You try to show to me
stuff I can never see:
The stocks, the weather, and
Granddaughter in the band,
and puppy in her lap.
(He needs a bigger ap.)

And you can map the stars,
and navigate to Mars,
and track our huntin' dog,
and listen while you jog.

Or you could learn Chinese,
or Dutch or Portuguese,
or with amazing ease,
you could call overseas.

It plays a tune and then
it's time to talk to Lynn.
It does a little hum;
your turn at Scrabble's come.

I know I can't compete.
Your social life's complete.
One thing it doesn't do
is pay its bill for you.

I'd throw your phone away
except I know you'd say:
"It's time to upgrade to
4G." It's calling you.

Smart Phone
Saves the Day

You brought your smart-ass phone
along to Yellowstone.
It beeped and booped and bopped,
the Scrabble never stopped.
But then your camera jammed,
and, Honey, I'll be damned,
you whipped your smart phone out
and photographed the route:
head-butting buffalo,
and geysers in the snow,
and travelers we met
we'd otherwise forget.
I hear the waterfalls.
I hear the mating calls.

Apologies to you,
and to your smart phone too.

The Quetzal Song

If I were a lonely Quetzal,
questing along on the breeze,
I'd search for another Quetzal
in all the jungle trees.
We'd find a Quetzal hostel
with a front door and a back,
and each would face the other way
to guard against attack.

If we were a Quetzal couple,
we'd raise some Quetzal chicks.
We'd feed them worms and berries
and giant Jaguar ticks.
Our chicks would grow up quickly.
We'd measure them each day.
And when their tails were long enough,
they all would fly away.

Fly my little Quetzals,
above the Mayan ruins,
above the mountain jungles;
go learn the village tunes.
Go see the coffee growing,
and the Amatitlan Lake,
but don't leave Guatemala,
or your little hearts will break.

If I were an ancient Quetzal, with
a crack and a chip in my beak,

I'd perch in an old banana tree
over a jungle creek.
I'd peck at a ripe banana,
soft enough to chew;
and nap away the afternoon,
and dream, my dear, of you.

The Poems

Made in the USA
Middletown, DE
01 July 2018